Printed in Great Britain
by Amazon.co.uk, Ltd.,
Marston Gate.

I believe that it is unwise to get between a dog and a fire hydrant.

- Burr Brown, dog lover and humorist

Table of Contents

Repartee

"You have seen people riding horses, but have you ever seen people ride dogs?"

"I did. 50 on a Greyhound."

"I want you to keep that dog out of the house. It's full of fleas."

"Fido! Don't go in the house. It's full of fleas!"

"I know a dog worth $10,000."

"How could a dog save so much?"

"Did you put the dog out?"

"Why? Is he on fire?"

"Why is your dog staring at me like that?"

"Probably because you're eating from his dish."

"Do you know that your dog barked all night?"

"Yes, but don't worry. He sleeps all day."

"I like this dog but his legs are too short."

"Too short? They reach the floor, don't they?"

"You must not pull that dog's tail!"

"I'm only holding it. The dog is pulling!"

One-Liners

I had a lap dog, but I had to get rid of him. Every time I sat on his lap he bit me.

One dog said to another: "What happened to me shouldn't happen to a man."

Stories that dogs can talk are't untrue. If any dog says he can talk, he's lying.

I have a fine watch dog. At any suspicious noise I wake the dog and he barks.

He is a Doberman Pincher. All day he goes around pinching Dobermans.

My dog is a lousy bloodhound. I cut my hand once and he fainted.

He's a very smart dog. In only two weeks he taught me how to give a paw.

Some dogs are pointers; mine is a nudger. He's too polite to point.

We got a dachshund so that all the children could pet him at the same time.

I've hated dogs ever since I went to a masquerade ball as a lamp post.

A barking dog never bites... while barking.

A dog is cheaper than a wife. The license is less and she already has a fur coat.

I have to get my dog a present or he'll bite my husband, again.

I got this dog for my wife. I wish I could make a trade like that every day.

My dog is afraid of burglars. I had to put an alarm system in his dog house.

Perhaps it's only a coincidence, but man's best friend can't talk.

He made his dog sit in the sun. He wanted to get a hot dog.

I call my dog 'Photographer' because he is always snapping people.

If a man bites a dog, he's probably eating a Frankfurter.

A Dachshund is a dog who wags his tail by remote control.

Dogs in Siberia are the fastest in the world because the trees are so far apart.

A country dog comes to the city and seeing his first parking meter thinks,
"How do you like that...PAY TOILETS!"

If you mated a Bulldog and a Shitsu, would it be called a Bullshit?

Why does Goofy stand erect while Pluto remains on all fours?

My dog can talk. I asked him what two minus two was and he said nothing.

Dogs are lousy poker players. With a good hand they wag their tails.

I was the teacher's pet. She couldn't afford a dog.

My dog is a bird dog, but I've never heard him sing.

I bought a dog whistle. He won't use it.

Did you ever notice that when you blow in a dog's face,

he gets mad at you,

but when you take him on a car ride,

he sticks his head out the window?

Long Dog Tails

Killer Chihuahua

A man walks into a bar one day and asks, "Does anyone here own that Rottweiler outside?"

"Yeah, I do!" a biker says, standing up. "What about it?"

"Well, I think my Chihuahua just killed him..."

"What are you talkin' about?!" the biker says, disbelievingly. "How could your little runt kill my Rottweiler?"

"Well, it seems he got stuck in your dog's throat!"

Ay, Chihuahua!

The Taco Bell Chihuahua, a Doberman, and a Bulldog are in a doggie bar

having a cool one when a good-looking female Belgian Tervuren comes up to

them and says, "Whoever can say liver and cheese in a sentence can have me."

So the Doberman says, "I love liver and cheese."

The Belgian says, "That's not good enough."

The Bulldog says, "I hate liver and cheese."

She says, "That's not creative."

Finally, the Chihuahua says, "Liver alone...cheese mine!"

Another Very Smart Dog!

I went to the cinema the other day and in the front row was an old man and with him was his dog. It was a sad, funny kind of film, you know the type. In the sad part, the dog cried his eyes out, and in the funny part, the dog laughed its head off. This happened all the way through the film. After the film ended, I decided to go and speak to the man.

"That's the most amazing thing I've seen," I said.

"That dog really seemed to enjoy the film."

The man turned to me and said, "Yeah, he did. He hated the book."

Another Very Smart Dog!

A man went to visit a friend and was amazed to find him playing chess with his dog. He watched the game in astonishment for a while."I can hardly believe my eyes!" he exclaimed. "That's the smartest dog I've ever seen."

"Nah, he's not so smart," the friend replied. "I've beaten him three games out of five."

Spike

Mrs. Davidson's dishwasher quit working, so she called a repairman but he couldn't accommodate her with an evening appointment. Since she had to go to work the next day, she told him: "I'll leave the key under the mat. Fix the dishwasher, leave the bill on the counter, and I'll mail you the check. By the way, don't worry about my Doberman, Spike. He won't bother you, but whatever you do...do NOT under any circumstances talk to my parrot!"

When the repairman arrived the next day, he discovered the biggest and meanest looking Doberman he had ever seen. But, just as she said, the dog just lay there on the carpet, watching the repairman go about his business. However, the whole time he was there, the parrot drove him nuts with his incessant yelling, cursing, and name-calling. Finally, the repairman couldn't contain himself any longer and yelled: "Shut up, you stupid ugly bird!"

To which the parrot replied: "Get him, Spike."

The Case for Soap and Water

A minister was asked to dinner by one of his church members. He knew she was a bad housekeeper but agreed nonetheless. When he sat down at the table, he noticed that the dishes were the dirtiest that he had ever seen in his life. "Were these dishes ever washed?" he asked his hostess, running his fingers over the grit and grime.

She replied, "They're as clean as soap and water could get them."

He felt a bit uncomfortable, but blessed the food anyway and started eating. It was really delicious and he said so, despite the dirty dishes.

When dinner was over, the hostess took the dishes outside and yelled,

"Here Soap! Here Water!"

Kung-Fu Poodle

Harold's new job had him working late hours. He thought to himself, "I should really get my wife a watch dog." So, he went to the pet store and asked for a Doberman.

The sales clerk responded, "If it's a guard dog that you want, I have a dog just for you!" He walked to the back of the store to get a dog and returned with a little poodle.

Harold exclaimed, "This small thing, a watch dog? You're kidding, right?"

The sales clerk answered, "No, this dog is special; he knows karate."

"Karate! I don't believe it," said Harold.

The salesman put the dog down and said, "Karate the sign!" as he pointed to a sign advertising dog food.

The dog ran up and ripped the sign to shreds. Harold was astounded.

Then the salesman said, "Karate the chair!" as he pointed to a chair in the corner. The dog ran up and ripped the chair to shreds.

By now Harold was thoroughly convinced that this was the dog he wanted. "I'll take him!" he declared.

When he arrived home he surprised his wife. She exclaimed, "This little thing, a watch dog? No way!"

Harold replied earnestly, "But this dog knows karate!"

"Karate?" she yelled. "Karate my arse!"

Lethal Injection

Three dogs, a Doberman, a Boxer, and a Lab are sitting in the vet's waiting room. The Doberman turns to the Boxer and asks, "So, why are you here?"

The Boxer replies, "I'm a pisser. I piss on everything - the sofa, the cat, and the kids. Last night I pissed in the middle of my owner's bed."

The Doberman says, "So what is the vet going to do?"

"Lethal injection," came the reply from the sad Boxer.

The Doberman then turns to the Labrador and asks, "Why are you here?

"The Lab says, "I'm a digger. I dig under fences, dig up flowers, and I dig just for the hell of it. Inside, I dig up carpets. Last night I dug a hole in my owner's couch."

"So what are they going to do to you?" the Doberman inquired.

"Lethal injection," the dejected Lab said. The Labrador then turns to the Doberman and asks what he's at the vet's office for."

"I'm a humper," the Doberman says. "I'll hump anything. I'll hump the cat, a pillow, the table, whatever. I want to hump everything I see. Yesterday, my owner got out of the shower and was bending down to dry her toes, and I couldn't help myself. I hopped on her back and started humping away."

The Boxer said, "So, lethal injection for you, too, huh?"

The Doberman says, "No, no, I'm here to get my nails clipped."

Killer

A man was leaving a cafe when he noticed an unusual funeral procession. A long black hearse was followed by a second long black hearse, followed by a solitary man walking a Pit Bull on a leash. Behind him was a queue of about 200 men or more walking in single file.

The man was so curious, he approached the man with the dog. "I am so sorry for your loss, and I know now this is a bad time to disturb you, but I've never seen a funeral like this. Whose funeral is it?"

The man replied, "Well, that first hearse is for my wife."

"What happened to her?"

The man replied, "My dog attacked and killed her."

He inquired further, "Well, who is in the second hearse?"

The man answered, "My mother-in-law. She was trying to help my wife when the dog turned on her."

A poignant and thoughtful moment of silence passed between the two men. "Can I borrow the dog?"

"Join the queue," the man replied.

Fluffy

This guy comes home from work one day to find his dog with the neighbor's pet rabbit in his mouth. The rabbit is very dead, and the guy panics.

He thinks the neighbors are going to hate him forever, so he takes the dirty, chewed-up rabbit into the house, gives it a bath, blow-dries its fur, and puts the rabbit back into the cage at the neighbor's house, hoping that they will think it died of natural causes.

A few days later, the neighbor is outside and asks the guy, "Did you hear that Fluffy died?" The guy stumbles around and says, "Um.. no.. um.. what happened?"

The neighbor replies, "We just found him dead in his cage one day, but the weird thing is that the day after we buried him we went outside and someone had dug him up, gave him a bath and put him back into the cage. There must be some real sick people out there!"

Watch Dog

Mr. Green had recently bought a dog and was proudly demonstrating his good points to a friend. "It's a very good dog," he said. "No tramp or beggar can come near the house without his letting us know about it."

"What does he do?" asked his friend. "Does he bark the house down?"

"Not at all," answered Mr. Green. "He crawls under the armchair."

How Many Dogs Does it Take to Change a Lightbulb?

Dachshund: You know I can't reach that stupid lamp!

Rottweiler: Make me.

Shi-tzu: Puh-leeze, dah-ling. Let the servants. . . .

Lab: Oh, me, me!!! Pleeeeeeze let me change the light bulb! Can I? Can I?

Malamute: Let the Border Collie do it. You can feed me while he's busy.

Jack Russell: I'll just pop it in while I'm bouncing off the walls.

Cocker Spaniel: Why change it? I can still pee on the carpet in the dark.

Doberman Pinscher: While it's dark, I'm going to sleep on the couch.

Boxer: Who cares? I can still play with my squeaky toys in the dark.

Mastiff: Mastiffs are NOT afraid of the dark.

Chihuahua: Yo quiero Taco Bulb.

Irish Wolfhound: Can somebody else do it? I've got this hangover...

Pointer: I see it, there it is, there it is, right there...

Greyhound: It isn't moving. Who cares?

Australian Shepherd: First, I'll put all the light bulbs in a little circle...

Old English Sheep Dog: Light bulb? That thing I just ate was a light bulb?

Westie: Dogs do not change light bulbs. People change light bulbs, I am not one of THEM, so the question is, how long will it be before I can expect my light?

Hound: ZZZZZZZZZZZZzzzzzzzzzzzzz

Cat: You need light to see?

Parrot Story

A burglar breaks into a house and shines his torch along the pitch-dark passage. Out of the darkness comes a voice saying, "Jesus is watching you."

He goes into the living room and the voice repeats the message,

"Jesus is watching you".

He shines the torch on a parrot on a perch, and says "What's your name?"

"My name is Polly" says the parrot.

"Then who on earth is Jesus?" asks the burglar.

"Jesus is the Rottweiler" - replies the parrot.

Q & A

Q: Why are dogs such poor dancers?

A: They have 2 left feet!

Q: Why do dogs turn around three times before lying down?

A: One good turn deserves another.

Q: Why do dogs bury bones in the ground?

A: Because you can't bury them in trees!

Q: Why did the poor dog chase his own tail?

A: He was trying to make both ends meet!

Q: What do you get if you cross a Sheepdog with a rose?

A: A collie-flower!

Q: What do you call a Russian vet?

A: "Chopabollockoff"

Q: Why do dogs wag their tails?

A: "Because no one else will do it for them!"

Q: Why didn't the dog speak to his foot?

A: Because it's not polite to talk back to your paw!

Q: What is the dogs' favorite city?

A: New Yorkie!

Q: Who is the dogs' favorite comedian?

A: Growlcho Marx!

Q: What did the cowboy say when the bear ate Lassie?

A: "Well, doggone!"

Q: What happened when the dog went to the flea circus?

A: He stole the show!

Q: How can you have a stupid dog?

A: It chases parked cars!

Q: What do you get if you take a really big dog out for a walk?

A: A Great Dane out!

Q: What do dogs have that no other animal has?

A: Puppy dogs!

Q: Why did the Dachshund bite the woman's ankle?

A: Because he was short and couldn't reach any higher!

Q: Where do Eskimos train their dogs?

A: In the mush room!

Q: Why did the snowman call his dog Frost?

A: Because frost bites!

Q: What do dogs and trees have in common?

A: Bark.

Q: Where do dogs get their pick'n'mix?

A: Wool-Woofs

Q: What do you get if you cross a giraffe with a dog?

A: An animal that barks at low flying aircraft!

Q: What do you call an alcoholic dog?

A: A whino!

Q: What is the difference between Father Christmas and a warm dog?

A: Father Christmas wears a whole suit, a dog just pants!

Q: When is the most likely time that a stray dog will walk into your house?

A: When the door is open!

Q: What do dogs and a penny have in common?

A: They both have heads and tails!

Q: What is a dog's favorite sport?

A: Formula 1 drooling!

Q: What do you get if you cross a dog with Concorde?

A: A jet setter!

Q: What kind of dog sounds like you can eat it?

A: Sausage dog!

Q: What do you do if your dog eats your pen?

A: Use a pencil instead!

Q: What do you get if you cross a dog and a cheetah?

A: A dog that chases cars - and catches them!

Q: What happens when it rains cats and dogs?

A: You can step in a poodle!

Q: What sort of clothes does a pet dog wear?

A: A petticoat!

Q: What do you get if you cross a dog and a lion?

A: A terrified postman!

Q: What happened to the dog who ate nothing but garlic?

A: His bark was much worse than his bite!

Q: What is a dog's favorite flower?

A: Anything in your garden!

Q: What dog wears contact lenses?

A: A cock-eyed spaniel!

Q: What's a dog favorite hobby?

A: Collecting fleas!

Q: What did the hungry Dalmatian say when he had a meal?

A: That hit the spots!

Q: What do you get if you cross a Rottweiler and a hyena?

A: I don't know but I'll join in if it laughs!

Q: Why do you need a license for a dog and not for a cat?

A: Cats can't drive!

Q: What do you call a dog in the middle of a muddy road?
A: A mutt in a rut!

Q: What do you get if you cross a dog with a blind mole?
A: A dog that keeps barking up the wrong tree!

Q: What do you call a happy Lassie?
A: A jolly Collie!

Q: What do you call a nutty dog in Australia?
A: A dingo-ling!

Q: What dog loves to take bubble baths?
A: A shampoodle!

Q: How do you catch a runaway dog?
A: Hide behind a tree and make a noise like a bone!

Q: What dogs are best for sending telegrams?
A: Wire-haired terriers!

Q: What kind of dog does a vampire prefer?
A: Any kind of bloodhound!

Q: Which dog is the most expensive of all?
A: Deer hound!

Q: What kind of dog sniffs out new flowers?
A: A bud hound!

Q: What kind of meat do you give a stupid dog
A: Chump chops

Q: How many seasons are there in a dog's life
A: Just one, the molting season!

Q: What do you call a dog with no legs?

A: It doesn't matter what you call him, he still won't come!

Q: Why is it called a "litter" of puppies?

A: Because they mess up the whole house!

Q: How do you stop a dog smelling?

A: Put a peg on it's nose!

Q: What is the best time to take a Rottweiler for a walk?

A: Any times he wants to!

Q: When is a black dog not a black dog?

A: When it's a Greyhound!

Q: How do you feel if you cross a Sheepdog with a melon?

A: Melon-collie!

Q: What do you get if cross two young dogs with a pair of headphones?

A: Hush puppies!

Dog Letters to God

Dear God,
Why do humans smell the flowers, but seldom, if
ever, smell one another?
Yours Truly,
Lily

Dear God,
When we get to heaven, can we sit on your couch?
Or is it the same old story?
Sincerely,
Gretchen

Dear God,
If a dog barks his head off in the forest and no
human hears him, is he still a bad dog?
Regards,
Lucy

Dear God,
We dogs can understand human verbal
instructions, hand signals, whistles, horns,
clickers, beepers, scent ID's, electromagnetic
energy fields, and Frisbee flight paths. What do
humans understand?
Respectfully,
Happy

Dear God,
Are there mailmen in Heaven? If there are, will I
have to apologize?
With all due respect,
Lady

Dear God,
May I have my testicles back?
Hopefully yours,
Mackie

Dear God,

Let me give you a list of twelve things I promise to remember to be a good dog:

1. I will not eat the cats' food before they eat it or after they throw it up.
2. I will not munch on 'leftovers' in the kitty litter box; although they are tasty, they are not food.
3. The garbage collector is not stealing our stuff.
4. My head does not belong in the refrigerator.
5. I will not bite the officer's hand when he reaches in for Mom's driver's license and registration.
6. I will not come in from outside and immediately drag my butt across the carpet.
7. I will not play tug-of-war with Dad's underwear when he's on the toilet.

8. Sticking my nose into someone's crotch is not
   an acceptable way of saying 'hello'.
9. I do not need to suddenly stand straight up
   when I'm lying under the coffee table.
10.I must shake the rainwater out of my fur
   before entering the house.
11. The empty seat at the dinning room table is
   not for me.
12. The cat is not a squeaky toy, so when I play
   with him and he makes that
   noise, it's usually not a good thing.
Honestly,
Rover

When Good Dogs Crossbreed, You Get...

- Pointer + Setter = **Poinsetter**, a traditional Christmas pet

- Kerry Blue Terrier + Skye Terrier = **Blue Skye**, a dog for visionaries

- Great Pyrenees + Dachshund = **Pyradachs**, a puzzling breed

- Pekingese + Lhasa Apso = **Peekasso**, an abstract dog

- Irish Water Spaniel + English Springer Spaniel = **Irish Springer**, a dog fresh and clean as a whistle

- Cocker Spaniel + Rottweiler = **Cockrot**, the perfect puppy for that philandering ex-husband

- Bull Terrier + Shitzu = **Bullshitz**, a gregarious but unreliable breed

- Newfoundland + Basset Hound = **Newfound Asset Hound**, a dog for financial advisors

- Terrier + Bulldog = **Terribull**, a dog prone to awful mistakes

- Bloodhound + Labrador = **Blabador**, a dog that barks incessantly

- Malamute + Pointer = **Moot Point**, owned by....oh, well, it doesn't matter anyway

- Collie + Malamute = **Commute**, a dog that travels to work

- Deerhound + Terrier = **Derriere,** a dog that's true to the end

- Cavalier + Airedale = **Caviar**, a very expensive British dog

- Labrador Retriever + Curly Coated Retriever = **Lab Coat Retriever**, the choice of research scientists

Dogs & Men

50 Reasons For A Girl To Choose A Dog... And Not A Man

1. Spots are an attractive feature on a dog.

2. A dog is better protection from intruders.

3. Dogs enjoy ball games. But they don't spend six hours on the phone trying to get tickets for the Superbowl.

4. Dogs greet each other by sniffing bottoms. Men are far less polite.

5. Puppy love doesn't wear off so quickly with a dog.

6. You can be prosecuted for neglecting a dog.

7. Dogs can find their way back home - even after a really heavy night out.

8. Dogs can be trained not to lie on the bed. Men always lie in bed.

9. A dog can molt without becoming obsessed about premature baldness.

10. Dogs can be taught the meaning of the word "NO!"

11. A dog is far less irritation to have in the back seat of a car...

12. ...and will be less likely to show its rear end to the people in the vehicle behind for a laugh.

13. Elizabeth Hurley has a faithful dog whom she loves dearly.

14. If a dog says sausages, that's clever. If a man says sausages, that's just greedy.

15. Dogs will wait patiently outside clothes' shops...

16. ... and not criticize your purchases afterwards.

17. A dog will fetch the morning paper for you.

18. A dog will trot faithfully round at your heel.

19. Dogs don't break wind in public and blame it on the man.

20. In the canine world, boxers are quite intelligent.

21. If a dog gets ill, it won't take eighteen Panadols in order to avoid having to go to the vet.

22. You can also ask the vet to perform the snip, even if the dog objects.

23. Small, ginger-haired dogs can be quite appealing. As for men? Two words. Robin Cook.

24. You can find a nice dog by advertising on a card in a shop window, or in the classified section of the local paper.

25. A woman can live with more than one dog, without rumors starting.

26. When dogs beg, it's cute. When men beg, it's pathetic.

27. Dogs sometimes dig the garden.

28. A dog can go out fox-hunting without being incredibly stuck up and pompous.

29. Dogs don't necessarily prefer blondes.

30. Dogs won't get embarrassed if you call them by a pet name when their friends are around.

31. Dogs travel more cheaply on the bus.

32. Dogs whine less.

33. Some dogs can be quite talented at singing.

34. Men lost the World Cup. A dog found it.

35. Dogs are less reliant on canned food...

36. ..but after a few cans, a dog will still be able to stand up.

37. And there are some things even a dog won't eat - like the remains of a three-day-old King Prawn vindaloo that they found on the floor behind the sofa.

38. You can leave a dog alone in your house without worrying so much about what it'll break.

39. A dog gets a new coat every winter.

40. Dogs are not so careless about leaving puddles on the bathroom floor.

41. A dog is less likely to leave a filthy, stinking mess for you to clear up.

42. For a dog, a wet nose is a sign of GOOD health.

43. Dogs don't leave the toilet seat up.

44. Dogs don't wolf-whistle.

45. There are still thousands of totally undomesticated dogs in Australia; but far more undomesticated men.

46. Your dog will never refer to you as 'a bitch'.

47. In disaster films, the dog is always far more likely to have a miraculous escape.

48. Dogs do not waste money betting on the dogs.

49. You can stop dogs getting too randy by throwing a bucket or water over them.

50. A 'King Charles' is much more likely to be a big, floppy-eared dog than a big floppy-eared man.

12 Ways Dogs And Men Are The Same

1. Both take up too much space on the bed.

2. Both have irrational fears about vacuum cleaning.

3. Both mark their territory.

4. Neither tells you what's bothering them.

5. The smaller ones tend to be more nervous.

6. Both have an inordinate fascination with women's crotches.

7. Neither does any dishes.

8. Both fart shamelessly.

9. Neither of them notice when you get your hair cut.

10. Both like dominance games.

11. Both are suspicious of the postman.

12. Neither understands what you see in cats.

Dog Philsophy

Eight Maxims For Dogs

1. If you stare at someone long enough, eventually you'll get what you want.

2. Don't go out without an ID.

3. Be direct with people; let them know exactly how you feel by pissing on their shoes.

4. Be aware of when to hold your tongue, and when to use it.

5. Leave room in your schedule for a good nap.

6. Always give people a friendly greeting. A cold nose in the crotch is most effective.

7. When you do something wrong, always take responsibility (as soon as you're dragged shamefully out from under the bed).

8. If it's not wet and sloppy, it's not a real kiss

Nine Things Dogs Just Don't Understand

1. It's not a laugh to practice barking at 3 a.m.

2. It's wrong to back Grandma into a corner and guard her.

3. He shouldn't jump on your bed when he's sopping wet.

4. The cats have every right to be in the living room.

5. Barking at guests 10 minutes after they arrive is stupid.

6. Getting up does NOT mean we are going for a walk.

7. Just because I'm eating, doesn't mean you can.

8. If you look at me with those big soppy eyes, I'm not going to give in and feed you. NO NO NO. Oh, ok, just this once.

9. No, it's my food....Oh alright then, just a small piece.

Ten Dog Property Laws

1. If I like it, it's mine.

2. If it's in my mouth, it's mine.

3. If I can take it from you, it's mine.

4. If I had it a little while ago, it's mine.

5. If it's mine, it must never appear to be yours in any way.

6. If I'm chewing something up, all the pieces are mine.

7. If it just looks like mine, it's mine.

8. If I saw it first, it's mine.

9. If it's broken, it's yours.

10. If you are playing with something and you put it down, it's automatically mine.

75

Quotations

"A few weeks after my surgery, I went out to play catch with my golden retriever. When I bent over to pick up the ball, my prosthesis fell out. The dog snatched it, and I found myself chasing him down the road yelling,"Hey, come back here with my breast!"
- Linda Ellerbee

"If you want to be liked, get a dog.
The people you work with are not your friends."
- Deborah Norville

"Speak softly and own a big, mean Doberman."
- Dave Miliman

"One reason the dog has so many friends:
He wags his tail instead of his tongue."
- Anon

"If you pick up a starving dog and make him prosperous, he will not bite you; that is the principal difference between a dog and a man."
- Mark Twain

> "Here, Gentlemen, a dog teaches us a lesson in humanity."
> - Napoleon Bonaparte

"To his dog, every man is Napoleon; hence the constant popularity of dogs."
- Aldous Leonard Huxley

> "We named the DOG Indiana!"
> - Henry Jones, Sr. (Sean Connery)
> Indiana Jones and the Last Crusade

"Cave canum (beware of the dog)."
- Anon

"It's not the size of the dog in the fight, it's the size of the fight in the dog."
- Mark Twain

"Ever consider what dogs must think of us? I mean, here we come back from a
grocery store with the most amazing haul -- chicken, pork,
half a cow. They must think we're the greatest hunters on earth!"
- Anne Tyler

"Beware of silent dogs and still waters."
- Portuguese Proverb

"Some days you're the dog, and some days you're the hydrant."
- Anon

"Never trust a dog to watch your food."
- Anon

"Heaven goes by favor. If it went by merit, you would stay out and your dog would go in."
- Mark Twain

"You can say any foolish thing to a dog, and the dog will give you a look that says, 'My God, you're right! I never would've thought of that!'"
- Dave Barry

"Artists like cats, soldiers like dogs."
- Desmond Morris

"Women and cats will do as they please, and men and dogs should relax and get used to the idea."
- Robert A. Heinlein

"I like pigs. Dogs look up to us. Cats look down on us. Pigs treat us as equals."
- Sir Winston Churchill

"It's easy to understand why the cat has eclipsed the dog as modern America's favorite pet. People like pets to possess the same qualities they do. Cats are irresponsible and recognize no authority, yet are completely dependent on others for their material needs. Cats cannot be made to do anything useful. Cats are mean for the fun of it."
- P. J. O'Rourke

"Cats are smarter than dogs.
You can't get eight cats to pull a sled through the snow."
- Jeff Valdez

"Dogs come when they're called; cats take a message and get back to you later."
- Mary Bly

"A dog has the soul of a philosopher."
- Plato

"To a dog the whole world is a smell."
- Anon

"Dogs wait for us faithfully."
- Marcus Tullius Cicero

"Dogs are not our whole life, but they make our lives whole."
- Roger Caras

"If you think dogs can't count, try putting three dog biscuits in your pocket and then giving Fido only two of them."
- Phil Pastorate

"If you are a dog and your owner suggests that you wear a sweater. . . suggest that he wear a tail."
- Fran Leibowitz

A dog is the only thing on earth that loves you more than he loves himself.
-Josh Billings

"My goal in life is to be as good of a person my dog already thinks I am."
- Anon

"Scratch a dog and you'll find a permanent job."
- Franklin P. Jones

"Asking a writer what he thinks about criticism is like asking a lamppost what it feels about dogs."
- John Osborne

"Don't accept your dog's admiration as conclusive evidence that you are wonderful."
-Ann Landers

"If there are no dogs in Heaven, then when I die I want to go where they went."
- Will Rogers

"A dog teaches a boy fidelity, perseverance, and to turn around three times before lying down."
- Robert Benchley

"The average dog is a nicer person than the average person."
- Andy Rooney

"Dogs love their friends and bite their enemies, quite unlike people, who are incapable of pure love and always have to mix love and hate."
- Sigmund Freud

"I wonder if other dogs think poodles are members of a weird religious cult."
- Rita Rudner

"Dogs need to sniff the ground; it's how they keep abreast of current events. The ground is a giant dog newspaper, containing all kinds of late-breaking dog news items, which, if they are especially urgent, are often continued in the next yard."
- Dave Barry

"If I have any beliefs about immortality, it is that certain dogs I have known will go to heaven, and very, very few persons."
- James Thurber

"My dog is worried about the economy because Alpo is up to $3.00 a can. That's almost $21.00 in dog money."
- Joe Weinstein

Man is a dog's idea of what God should be.
- Anon

"We give dogs time we can spare, space we can spare and love we can spare. And in return, dogs give us their all. It's the best deal man has ever made."
- M. Acklam

"No one appreciates the very special genius of your conversation as a dog does."
- Christopher Morely

"Money will buy you a fine dog, but only love can make it wag it's tail."
- Anon

"Things that upset a terrier may pass virtually unnoticed by a Great Dane."
- Anon

"There is only one smartest dog in the world, and everybody has it."
- Anon

"A dog is the only friend you can buy for money."
- Anon

"A woman's preaching is like a dog walking on its hind legs.
It's not done well but one's surprised to see it done at all".
- Samuel Johnson

"There is nothing like walking a dog
to make a person feel better off."
- Anon

"Whoever said you can't buy happiness forgot about little puppies."
- Gene Hill

"A dog is known as a man's best friend, because it gives no advice, never tries to borrow money and has no in-laws."
- Anon

"When a man's best friend is his dog, that dog has a problem."
- Edward Abbey

"Dogs feel very strongly that they should always go with you in the car, in case the need should arise for them to bark violently at nothing right in your ear."
- Dave Barry

"Of all the things I miss from veterinary practice,
puppy breath is one of the most fond memories!"
- Dr. Tom Cat

"In order to keep a true perspective of one's importance, everyone should
have a dog that will worship him and a cat that will ignore him."
- Dereke Bruce, Taipei, Taiwan

"You enter into a certain amount of madness
when you marry a person with pets."
- Nora Ephron

"Dogs love their friends and bite their enemies, quite unlike people,
who are incapable of pure love and always have to mix love and hate."
- Sigmund Freud

"No animal should ever jump up on the dining room furniture unless absolutely certain that he can hold his own in the conversation."
- Fran Leibowitz

"Outside of a dog, a book is probably man's best friend; inside of a dog, it's too dark to read."
- Groucho Marx

"No one appreciates the very special genius of your conversation as the dog does."
- Christopher Morley

"In dog years, I'm dead."
- Anon

"You know why dogs have no money? No pockets. 'Cause they see change on the street all the time and it's driving them crazy. When you're walking them. He is always looking up at you. 'There's a quarter...'"
- Jerry Seinfeld

"My neighbor has two dogs. One of them says to the other, 'Woof!.' The other replies, 'Moo!.' The dog is perplexed. 'Moo? Why did you say, "Moo?" The other dog says, "I'm trying to learn a foreign language."'
- Morey Amsterdam

"There are three faithful friends--an old wife, an old dog and ready money."
- Ben Franklin

"Life is like a dogsled team. If you ain't the lead dog,
the scenery never changes."
- Lewis Gizzard

"They say the dog is man's best friend. I don't believe that.
How many of your friends have you neutered?"
- Larry Reeb

"He that lieth down with dogs, shall rise up with fleas."
- Ben Franklin

"I have a great dog. She's half Lab, half pit bull. A good combination.
Sure, she might bite off my leg, but she'll bring it back to me."
- Jimi Celeste

"When you leave them in the morning, they stick their nose in the door crack and stand there like a portrait until you turn the key eight hours later."

- Erma Bombeck

"Every time I go near the stove, the dog howls."

- Phillis Diller

"I've been on so many blind dates I should get a free dog."

- Wendy Liebman

'My advice to any diplomat who wants to have good press is to have two or three kids and a dog."

- Carl Rowan

"They have dog food for constipated dogs. If your dog is constipated, why screw up a good thing? Stay indoors and let 'em bloat!"

- David Letterman

"I bought my grandmother a Seeing Eye dog. But he's a little sadistic. He does impressions of cars screeching to a halt."

-Larry Amoros

"I like driving around with my two dogs, especially on the freeways.

I make them wear little hats so I can use the car-pool lanes."

- Monica Piper

"Man is a dogs ideal of what God should be."

- Holbrook Jackson English Journalist

"Keep running after a dog and he will never bite you."

- Francois Rabelais, French Humorist.

"As who should say, I am Sir Oracle,
And when I open my lips, let no dog bark!"
- Gratiano, scene i, 'The Merchant of Venice,' William Shakespeare

"About the only thing on a farm that has an easy time is the dog."

- Edgar Watson Houe, American Journalist

"Histories are more full of examples of the
fidelity of dogs than of friends."
- Alexander Pope, English Poet

"Oh, that dog! Ever hear of a German shepherd that bites its nails?

Barks with a lisp? You say, "Attack!" And he has one. All he does is piddle.

He's nothing but a fur-covered kidney that barks."

- Phillis Diller

"A man bitten by a dog, whether the animal is mad or not,

is apt to get mad himself."

- George D. Prentice American Journalist & Humorist

"It was a small town: Ferguson, Ohio. When you entered there was a big sign
and it said, "Welcome to Ferguson. Beware of the Dog."

- Jackie Vernon

"Revenge is often like biting a dog

because the dog bit you."

- Austin O'Malley American Oculist

"I went to an exclusive kennel club. It was very exclusive.

A sign out front read: 'No Dogs Allowed.'"

- Phil Foster

"The more I see of the depressing stature of people,

the more I admire my dogs."

Alphonse de Lamartine 1790-1869 French Poet

"When there is an old maid in the house, a watchdog is unnecessary."
- Honore de Balzac, French Novelist

"Man is an animal that makes bargains; no other animal does this-
no dog exchanges bones with another."
- Adam Smith, Scottish Politician and Economist

"The man who gets bit twice by the same dog
is better adapted for that kind of business than any other."
- Josh Billings

"The more I see of men the more I like dogs."
- Madame de Stael 1766-1817 French social leader

"Ladies and gentlemen are permitted to have friends in the kennel but not in the kitchen."

- George Bernard Shaw, British Dramatist

"Heaven goes by favor; if it went by merit, you would stay out and your dog would go in."

- Mark Twain

"When a man's dog turns against him it is time for a wife to pack her trunk and go home to mama."

- Mark Twain

"A door is what a dog is perpetually on the wrong side of."

- Ogden Nash

"A reasonable amount of fleas is good for a dog; it keeps him from brooding over being a dog."

- Edward Noyes Westcott, American Banger & Novelist

"If dogs could talk, perhaps we'd find it just as hard to get along with them as we do people."

- Karel Capek, Czech Journalist

"I know that dogs are pack animals, but it is difficult to imagine a pack of standard poodles...and if there was such a thing as a pack of standard poodles, where would they rove to? Bloomingdale's?"

- Yvonne Clifford, American actress

"My little dog -- a heartbeat at my feet."

- Edith Wharton

"The poor dog, in life the firmest friend, the first to welcome, foremost to defend."

- Lord Byron, an epitaph for his dog Boatswain.

"A good dog never dies. He always stays. He walks besides you on crisp autumn days when frost is on the fields and winter's drawing near.

His head is within our hand in his old way."

- Mary Carolyn Davies

"Children and dogs are as necessary to the welfare of the country as Wall Street and the railroads."

- Harry S. Truman

"A dog is like an eternal Peter Pan, a child who never grows old and who therefore is always available to love and be loved."

- Aaron Katcher, American Educator and Psychiatrist

"She was such a beautiful and sweet creature... and so full of tricks."

- Queen Victoria

"Properly trained, a man can be dog's best friend."

- Corey Ford, American writer

"What kind of life a dog... acquires, I have sometimes tried to imagine by kneeling or lying full length on the ground and looking up. The world then becomes strangely incomplete: one sees little but legs."

- E.V. Lucas, English writer

"They never talk about themselves but listen to you while you talk about yourself, and keep up an appearance of being interested in the conversation."

- Jerome K. Jerome, English humorist

"Not Carnegie, Vanderbilt and Astor together could have raised money enough to buy a quarter share in my little dog."

- Ernest Thompson Seton, American writer and naturalist

"Acquiring a dog may be the only opportunity a human

ever has to choose a relative."

- Mordecai Siegal, Contemporary Writer

"Being patted is what it is all about."

- Roger Caras

"Bulldogs are adorable, with faces like toads that have been sat on."

-Anon

"My hounds are bred out of the Spartan kind; So flew'd, so sanded; their heads are hung with ears that sweep away the morning dew..."

- William Shakespeare, a Midsummer Night's Dream

"Sir, this is a unique dog. He does not live by tooth or fang. He respects the right of cats to be cats although he doesn't admire them. He turns his steps rather than disturb an earnest caterpillar. His greatest fear is that someone will point out a rabbit and suggest that he chase it. This is a dog of peace and tranquility."

-John Steinbeck

"Why is it that my heart is so touched whenever I meet a dog lost in our noisy streets? Why do I feel such anguished pity when I see one of these creatures coming and going, sniffing everyone, frightened, despairing of even finding its master?"

- Emil Zola

"They are better than human beings, because they know but do not tell."

- Emily Dickinson

"In the late summer afternoon, when the teacups were cleared, and the family went inside... the dogs who are no longer under human command, find delight in the company of each other."

- Joe Dunnea, Irish Writer

"God... sat down for a moment when the dog was finished in order to watch it... and to know that it was good, that nothing was lacking, that it could not have been made better."

- Rainer Maria Rilke

"Fifth Avenue is too expensive for anyone but dogs."

- Mel Finkelstein, Daily News

"Dogs are our link to paradise. They don't know evil or jealousy or discontent. To sit with a dog on a hillside on a glorious afternoon is to be back in Eden, where doing nothing was not boring -- it was peace."

- Milan Kundera

The Airedale... an unrivaled mixture of brains, and clownish wit, the very ingredients one looks for in a spouse.

- Chip Brown, Connoisseur Magazine

"The great pleasure of a dog is that you make a fool of yourself with him and not only will he not scold you, he will make a fool of himself too."

- Samuel Butler

"His name is not wild dog anymore, but the first friend, because he will be our friend for always and always and always."

- Rudyard Kipling

Some dogs live for praise they look at you as if to say "Don't throw balls... just throw bouquets."

- Jhordis Anderson, American Painter

"The Saluki... is a marvel of elegance."

-Vita Sackville-West

"The pug is living proof that God has a sense of humor."

- Margot Kaufman, American writer

"She had no particular breed in mind, no unusual requirements. Except the special sense of mutual recognition that tells dog and human they have both come to the right place."

- Lloyd Alexander, American writer

Parting Poems

Puggy-Wug

Oh, what is the matter with poor
      Puggy-Wug?
Pet him and kiss him and give him a hug.
Run and fetch him a suitable drug.
Wrap him up tenderly all in a rug.
That is the way to cure Puggy-Wug.

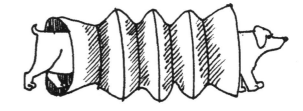

    - Winston Churchill
On his daughter Mary's pet Pug

"If a dog's prayers were answered, bones would rain from the sky."

- Old Proverb

Faithful

With eye upraised his master's look to scan,
The joy, the solace, and the aid of man;
The rich man's guardian and the poor man's friend,
The only creature faithful to the end.

- George Crabbe

Dima Yeremenko with George (left) and Teddy (right)
Photograph by Yulia Titovets

Dima Yeremenko, MSc

Dima Yeremenko is the author of *Dima's Dog School, The Foolproof New Way to Train Your Dog* and *Handfeeding Handbook: Five Easy Steps to a Well-Trained Happy Dog.*

Dima, often called the Dog Whisperer of London, is a Russian dog training instructor and behaviorist, as well as the owner of the Good Boy Dog School where he promotes responsible dog ownership, provides behavioral help and advice to people and families with dogs, gives dogs a good start in life, and tries to improve the lives of dogs with behavioral problems.

Over the years, Dima compiled the contents of this book... all in good fun!

Good Boy Dog School Session
Photograph by Yulia Titovets

Good Boy Dog School

The Good Boy Dog School is Dima Yeremenko's dog training school based in North London. It offers the whole range of services including one-to-one dog training and advice sessions, group dog training classes, home visits, residential training courses, sitting services, etc.

By providing both theoretical and practical help and assistance, the school is improving the lives of people's dogs starting as young as 8 weeks old to even some veterans as old.

"Old dogs do learn new tricks! But the most important for us - you do too."
- Dima Yeremenko

GoodBoyDogSchool.com • dimadogs@hotmail.com

Happy Lady Productions, LLC (HLP) is an independent, philanthropic publisher of non-fiction, fiction and children's picture books created by husband and wife team, photographer and photo illustrator Dan Merchant and writer Emily Randolph. HLP donates to charitable organizations supporting animal rescue and pet-therapy programs.

HappyLadyProductions.com • erandolph@happyladyproductions.com

DISCLAIMER

Every attempt has been made to make proper attribution to the jokes in this book.
We can only assume that the Internet, our greatest research tool, will occasionally fail us in its accuracy, and we apologize in advance for any errors.

Some Days You're the Dog...
Some Days, the Hydrant!

Compiled by Dima Yeremenko
Quips, Quotes & Jokes Overheard at the Good Boy Dog School

A proud endeavor of: